Contents

The Man with a Dream

It's a hot summer day in late August, and more than 200,000 people are standing in front of the Lincoln Memorial in Washington DC. In front of them, surrounded by microphones, is Dr Martin Luther King Jr.

King tells the crowd, 'I have a dream'. His dream is the end of racial prejudice – a day when all people will be judged equally, regardless of their race, religion or skin colour.

Martin Luther King speaking to crowds in Washington DC on 28 August, 1963.

'I have a dream that my four little children will one day live in a nation where they will not be judged by the color of their skin but by the content of their character. I have a dream today.'
Martin Luther King at the March on Washington.

Martin Luther King Jr
Civil Rights Hero

Anna Claybourne

HODDER
Wayland

an imprint of Hodder Children's Books

© 2001 White-Thomson Publishing Ltd

Produced by White-Thomson Publishing Ltd
2/3 St Andrew's Place, Lewes, BN7 1UP

Editor: Liz Gogerly
Cover Design: Jan Sterling
Inside Design: Joyce Chester
Picture Research: Shelley Noronha –
   Glass Onion Pictures
Proofreader: Alison Cooper

Cover: Martin Luther King inside Ebenezer Baptist Church,
in Atlanta, Georgia, 1964.

Published in Great Britain in 2001 by Hodder Wayland,
an imprint of Hodder Children's Books
This paperback edition published in 2002
Reprinted in 2003 and 2004

The right of Anna Claybourne to be identified as the author
of this Work has been asserted by her in accordance with
the Copyright, Designs and Patents Act 1988

British Library Cataloguing in Publication Data
Claybourne, Anna
   Martin Luther King: civil rights hero. – (Famous Lives)
   1. King, Martin Luther, 1929–1968
   2. Afro-American Civil rights workers – Biography
   3. Civil rights workers – United States
   I. Title II. Claybourne, Anna
   323.1'196'073'092

ISBN 0 7502 3884 4

Printed in China

Hodder Children's Books
An imprint of Hodder Headline Limited
338 Euston Road, London, NW1 3BH

Picture acknowledgements
The publisher would like to thank the following for giving
permission to use their pictures:
Corbis *cover*, 7, 8, 9, 10, 11, 12, 13, 14, 15, 16, 17, 22, 24,
26, 28, 31 (top and bottom), 32, 33, 34, 35, 36, 43;
HWPL 5 (top), 23, 24, 25 (top), 37, 38, 42 (left and
right); Photri Inc. 5 (bottom), 6, 27; Popperfoto 4, 19, 21,
25 (bottom), 30, 39 (top and bottom), 40, 45; Topham
Picturepoint / © Dinodia 10 (top), 18, 20, 29, 41, 44

Right: **Many black Americans had moved from the South to cities in the North. They were in search of a better life but found themselves in poor areas, like this black ghetto in Chicago.**

It was 1963, less than half a century ago. Yet until that time, if you were a black American, especially in the South, you were a second-class citizen. You had to live, eat, shop, work and go to school separately from whites. You also had to live with a constant threat of violence. This was the situation Martin Luther King had decided to change.

Only five years later, he lay dead, killed by an assassin's bullet. But for his attackers, it was too late. King and his followers had already changed the world.

Left: **A man drinks at a segregated (separate) water fountain for black people in the American South, early in the twentieth century.**

'As Good as Anyone'

Martin Luther King was born on 15 January 1929, in Atlanta, Georgia, in the heart of the American South. Like his father, a Baptist preacher, Martin's real name was Michael, not Martin. Both father and son were nicknamed Martin after Martin Luther, a famous sixteenth-century German religious reformer.

Martin Luther King's birthplace.

'You are as good as anyone.'
Alberta Williams King, King's mother.

The King family lived on Auburn Avenue, in a black area of Atlanta. They always had enough money to live on, and King later described his childhood as incredibly happy.

Yet he was puzzled by segregation — the system that forced black and white people to live their lives separately. From the 1500s to the 1800s, black people had been forced to work as slaves for whites. Slavery was abolished in 1865, but blacks were still treated as inferior and forced to use separate facilities.

King was upset when his best friend, a white boy, was told not to play with him any more, and he asked his mother why. She told him that although black people had to live with the segregation system, it did not reflect the real truth — that all people were equal and just as good as each other.

This picture from the 1860s shows black slaves from the state of Virginia as they work at the docks.

7

Unfair Treatment

King remembered his mother's words. He tried to remind himself that he was a 'somebody', not a 'nobody'. But as he grew older, he became more and more shocked by the way black people were treated.

On one occasion, a white woman slapped him for standing on her toe. Another time, he and his father were told to wait in the back of a shoe store, out of sight of the white customers. King also saw blacks being beaten by the Ku Klux Klan, a group who claimed white people were a superior race.

Members of the Ku Klux Klan, wearing white cloaks and hoods, confronting a group of black people in Florida in 1938.

He especially hated having to sit at the back of buses, and giving up his seat to whites. When he was fifteen, he took part in a public speaking contest in Dublin, Georgia. On the bus home, he and his teacher had to give up their seats. They stood up for 144 km (90 miles). King was so angry, he decided something had to change.

'*I would end up having to go to the back of that bus with my body, but every time I got on that bus I left my mind up on the front seat. And I said to myself, "One of these days I'm going to put my body up there where my mind is".*'
King recalling his daily bus trip to high school.

This photo was taken on a segregated bus in Texas. Black people were made to sit at the back.

College and Coretta

In 1944 King followed in his father's footsteps, and went to train as a preacher at Morehouse College. In 1948 he entered Crozer Theological Seminary and received a degree in sociology. But college gave King more than qualifications – it brought him excitement, and for the first time he could discuss the race issue freely.

At college, he thought hard about how to end racism. As a Christian, he had been taught to love and forgive his enemies. Yet he also believed in challenging racial injustice.

Martin Luther King, dressed in a cap and gown to receive one of his degrees.

'**His message was so profound and electrifying that I left the meeting and bought half-a-dozen books on Gandhi's life and works.'**
King, describing how he felt after hearing a lecture on Gandhi.

He was inspired by an Indian named Mahatma Gandhi. Gandhi had fought against British rule in India, not with violence, but by leading millions of people in peaceful protests. King was thrilled. He realized that blacks in the South could also use non-violent protests to fight segregation.

Above: *Gandhi (bare-legged) wore his simple white robe wherever he went.*

In 1951, King went to university in Boston, Massachusetts to study for a doctorate in theology. There, he fell in love with a clever, beautiful music student named Coretta Scott. In June 1953, when King was twenty-four, they were married. Coretta became a devoted partner who gave King the emotional support he needed for the work ahead of him.

Right: *Martin and Coretta were to remain happily married and deeply in love for the rest of Martin's life.*

A Minister in Montgomery

After college, King and Coretta moved back to the South, where King took up his first job. He was to be the new minister, or preacher, at Dexter Avenue Baptist Church in Montgomery, Alabama.

He also joined the Montgomery branch of the NAACP (National Association for the Advancement of Colored People) — an organization that campaigned for equal rights for blacks. A natural leader and brilliant public speaker, King was soon elected as one of its leaders.

King loved his work, and in November 1955 he and Coretta had their first baby, Yolanda Denise. They were overjoyed, and everything seemed perfect. Then, on 1 December 1955, something happened that was to turn their lives upside-down.

A portrait of Martin Luther King dressed in his cassock (minister's gown).

Rosa Parks, the secretary of the Montgomery NAACP, refused to give up her bus seat to a white man. The bus driver called the police, and she was arrested. The leaders of the NAACP decided this was the last straw. After paying the bond to rescue Rosa Parks from jail, they came up with a plan to boycott the buses.

Right: **Rosa Parks, who stood up for her rights by staying in her seat on a bus instead of giving it up when she was told to.**

'We have taken this type of thing too long already,' Nixon concluded, his voice trembling. 'I feel that the time has come to boycott the buses.' King, recalling a phone conversation with his friend E. D. Nixon, a senior NAACP member.

The Montgomery Bus Boycott

King with his wife and supporters during the Montgomery bus boycott.

On the night of Friday, 2 December, Montgomery's black ministers and leaders held a meeting in King's church. They agreed to send out thousands of leaflets urging Montgomery's black population not to use the buses. Instead, they should walk or share cars to get to work and school.

On Monday morning, King and Coretta were amazed to see a bus driving past their house, completely empty. The leaflets had worked!

The black leaders met up again that afternoon and formed a new organization to run the protest. They named it the Montgomery Improvement Association, or MIA, and elected King as its president.

That night, TV cameras, reporters and thousands of black protesters turned up to a mass meeting. As MIA leader, King made a powerful speech urging the people to stick to their boycott. It was an early example of the amazing speechmaking skills which would make him world-famous. As he finished, the building resounded with cheers.

'We are not wrong in what we are doing ... If we are wrong, God Almighty is wrong ... And we are determined here in Montgomery to work and fight until justice runs down like water and righteousness like a mighty stream.'
King at the MIA meeting at Holt Street Baptist Church, 5 December 1955.

From December 1955 the buses in Montgomery were virtually empty as people found other ways of getting to work. As well as walking, people used horse-drawn carts or mules.

15

The Backlash Begins

King urges people to remain calm as he stands in his porch after the bomb attack. To his right stands Montgomery's fire chief, R. L. Lampley and Mayor W.A.Gayle (in uniform), and to his left stands the city police commissioner, Clyde Sellers.

The bus company started losing money fast as, day after day, black people refused to ride on the buses.

The local government and police force were outraged. They began a 'get tough' campaign, trying to halt the boycott by arresting as many black drivers as they could for imaginary traffic offences.

But worse was to come. On 30 January, a bomb went off on the porch of King's house, when Coretta and Yolanda were inside. They weren't harmed, but the bombing worried King. He told the crowds outside that no one should seek revenge. Their protest was non-violent, and it had to stay that way.

Eventually, the police decided that the boycott was against the law, and they arrested King and many of the other protesters. The protesters responded by laughing and singing in the jail. In March 1956, when King was found guilty of leading an illegal boycott, he came out of the courtroom laughing and celebrating.

'Ordinarily, a person leaving a courtroom with a conviction behind him would wear a somber face. But I left with a smile. I knew that I was a convicted criminal, but I was proud of my crime.'
King on being convicted of leading an illegal boycott in 1956.

Coretta Scott King smiling with her husband as he emerges from the courtroom after his trial on boycott charges.

Victory!

The Montgomery bus boycott held out. For almost a year, people shared cars or walked distances of up to 20 km (12 miles) to work. Desperate for a solution, the city government decided that sharing cars was also illegal. On 13 November 1956, King and several others were again put on trial.

As they sat in the court, a reporter came running up to King with some important news. The US Supreme Court had ruled that bus segregation in Alabama was unconstitutional. This meant it was against the USA national laws, and would have to be abolished.

On 21 December, King took his first desegregated bus ride, sitting near the front of a bus next to a white preacher friend, Glenn Smiley.

King riding on a desegregated bus with black and white friends after the Montgomery victory.

'The bus driver greeted me with a cordial smile. As I put my fare in the box he said, "I believe you are Reverend King, aren't you?" I answered "Yes I am." "We are glad to have you this morning," he said.'
Martin Luther King remembering his first desegregated bus ride.

The movement for civil rights (equal rights for all races) now took off, as other towns across the South began similar boycotts and campaigns. Meanwhile the federal (national) government began to enforce desegregation in schools. King was disappointed that black students in Little Rock, Arkansas had to go to school under the protection of federal troops but he recognized that to enforce law and order this had been necessary. Above everything, King still believed in non-violence.

Federal guards escort black children into a newly desegregated school in Little Rock, Arkansas, in 1957.

Travels Abroad

Around the world, many Asian and African nations were breaking away and becoming independent from the European countries that had once ruled them.

As news of the civil rights struggle in the USA spread, many people in these newly independent lands saw King as a hero. He was invited on official visits to India and to Ghana, in West Africa.

In Ghana, King witnessed the birth of a new nation as Britain handed over control to the new prime minister, Kwame Nkrumah.

Ghana's new leader, Dr Kwame Nkrumah, waves to the crowd at Ghana's independence celebrations, which King attended in 1957.

In India, King and his wife visited villages where they met untouchables – the people at the bottom of India's caste system. The government was trying to introduce equal rights, but untouchables still did all the worst jobs and were treated badly by the rest of society.

King saw that black people in the USA were like the untouchables. His travels inspired him to keep fighting for equal rights for everyone – not just in the USA, but around the globe.

King and his wife meeting India's first Prime Minister, Jawaharlal Nehru, on a visit to India in 1959.

'And I said to myself, "Yes, I am an untouchable, and every Negro in the USA is an untouchable".'
King describing his trip to India in a sermon in Atlanta in 1965.

A Brush with Death

King had written a book about the Montgomery bus boycott, called *Stride Toward Freedom*. He was in a New York department store signing copies, when a stranger plunged a razor-sharp paper-knife into his chest.

King underwent a huge operation to remove the knife. The doctors said that the blade had been touching a major artery. If he had sneezed before the operation, it would have pierced the artery and he would have died.

Dear Dr. King,
I am a ninth-grade student at the White Plains High School. While it should not matter, I would like to mention that I am a white girl. ... And I'm simply writing you to say that I'm so happy that you didn't sneeze.
A letter of support sent to King in 1958, after he was stabbed in New York.

The attacker was not an assassin, but a mentally ill black woman named Izola Ware Curry. However, King's family and friends were plagued by other violent attacks. His friend Ralph Abernathy's home and church were bombed, and a burning cross was left in King's garden as a threat from the Ku Klux Klan.

This atmosphere of violence made King surer than ever that non-violent protests were the only way ahead. He urged all black campaigners to love their enemies and to keep their protests peaceful at all times.

King, with his second child, Martin Luther King III, looks at a burnt cross left in his garden by the Ku Klux Klan.

The Movement Grows

King had been elected leader of a new civil rights organization called the Southern Christian Leadership Conference, or SCLC. By 1960, his work for the SCLC was taking up almost all of his time.

Reluctantly, he decided to leave Montgomery. He moved back to Atlanta with his family to work part-time in his father's church, so that he could spend more time on the struggle.

King at home in Atlanta in 1960 with Coretta, Yolanda and his second child, Martin Luther King III.

That year, the civil rights movement turned into a revolution. Students across the South staged sit-ins at segregated lunch counters, stores and cafés. They aimed to get themselves arrested and fill up the jails until their demands for equality were met. They endured police attacks and threats from the Ku Klux Klan.

Left: *Students stage a sit-in at a restaurant in Oklahoma City.*

'*Commit yourself to the noble struggle for equal rights. You will make a greater person of yourself, a greater nation of your country, and a finer world to live in.*'
King speaking to students at an integrated high school in 1959.

Below: *President Kennedy meets King, Ray Wilkins (head of NAACP) and Dorothy Height (President of the National Council of Negro Women) in Washington DC in 1962.*

But the federal government supported the struggle. A Democratic senator named John F. Kennedy spoke up for King, and helped arrange his release after he had been arrested in Atlanta.

Birmingham: The Big One

In 1962, the SCLC agreed to launch a new civil rights campaign in Birmingham, Alabama. Birmingham was, according to King, 'the most thoroughly segregated city in America'. Yet he knew that if they could succeed there, the civil rights movement would soon be unstoppable.

The SCLC organized a huge schedule of sit-ins, marches and boycotts. The police responded with fire hoses, dogs and clubs. The jails were filled with between four and five hundred protesters, including King, who was arrested on 12 April, Good Friday, 1963.

While he was in prison King read a newspaper article which moved him to write his Letter from Birmingham Jail. In the article, seven Christian clergymen and a rabbi had criticized the SCLC. In his letter King justified the work of the SCLC and expressed his disappointment that religious leaders in the South had done little for civil rights.

King and his friend Ralph Abernathy leading a protest march in Birmingham, Alabama.

> *'For years now I have heard the word "Wait!" It rings in the ears of every Negro with piercing familiarity. This "Wait" has almost always meant "Never".'*
> Part of King's Letter from Birmingham Jail, which he wrote after white preachers in Birmingham called on him to end the protests and wait for equality.

After his release, King organized more protests, including a march of thousands of children. After just six weeks of protests, the local politicians gave in, and agreed on an equal rights plan.

There were violent reprisals – King's motel and his brother's house were bombed. But John F Kennedy – now the US president sent federal troops to enforce the new, desegregated system.

Families protesting against segregation in schools outside a School Board office in Birmingham, Alabama.

27

March on Washington

After the Birmingham campaign, in June 1963, President Kennedy announced proposals for a new civil rights bill. That summer was filled with an atmosphere of joy and success, and protesters adopted the slogan 'Free in '63'.

A. Philip Randolph, one of the civil rights leaders, had an idea for a massive public march and rally in Washington DC, the capital city of the USA. It was arranged for 28 August 1963.

'...all of God's children, black men and white men, Jews and Gentiles, Protestants and Catholics, will be able to join hands and sing in the words of the old Negro spiritual: "Free at last! Free at last! Thank God Almighty, we are free at last!"'
The ending of King's famous address at the March on Washington, also known as the 'I have a dream' speech.

On that day, over 200,000 people of all races and faiths went to Washington to declare their support for civil rights. There, they heard Martin Luther King deliver one of the most famous speeches of all time – his 'I have a dream' speech.

King later said that he had prepared a speech, but had left it aside halfway through. His famous words about his dream of complete equality were improvised.

King and Coretta with three of their four children. This photograph was taken when five-year-old Martin Luther King III (left) had just been turned down by a school to which he had applied.

Violence Erupts

Sadly, the joy and hope of the summer of 1963 were short-lived. Two weeks after the Washington march, the racists of Birmingham took their revenge. They blew up the Sixteenth Street Baptist Church, where many black people worshipped, during a service. Four young girls were killed.

King spoke at the funeral of three of the girls, determined as ever that the non-violent struggle had to continue. He hoped that the horror of the crime would shame white Southerners into abandoning racism and accepting the need for love and equality between all people.

'We are more determined than ever before that non-violence is the way. Let them bring on their bombs ... We intend to be free.' King after the bombing of a church in Birmingham in September 1963.

The Sixteenth Street Baptist Church in Birmingham, Alabama after it was bombed by terrorists in 1963, killing four children.

Above: **By 1963, King had many supporters, both black and white.**

Right: **Whites beat up a black man in Jackson, Mississippi in 1963.**

Yet that November, there was another shock. President Kennedy, who had been such a strong supporter of civil rights, was shot dead by an assassin while visiting Dallas, Texas.

King did not believe that Kennedy's killing could have been an isolated act. He blamed it on the whole culture of hatred and violence which he saw pervading America.

The Civil Rights Act

'This legislation was first written in the streets. The epic thrust of the millions of Negroes who demonstrated in 1963 in hundreds of cities won strong white allies to the cause. Together they created a "coalition of conscience".'
King on the Civil Rights Act of 1964.

Martin Luther King with President Johnson at the signing of the Civil Rights Act on 2 July, 1964.

Before his death, President Kennedy had introduced a new civil rights bill, outlawing segregated housing and education. While the civil rights struggle continued across the South, the federal government considered the new bill. In July 1964, it was passed.

King welcomed the Civil Rights Act as a historic moment. As the leading light of the movement, he was invited to attend the signing of the act.

King at the start of a civil rights march in Alabama in 1965.

After writing his signature, President Lyndon Johnson gave King the pen he had used. King later wrote that it was among his most treasured possessions.

But although the act made equality the law, King knew prejudice would not end overnight. Black people still had the worst jobs and the worst pay. He resolved to fight on.

The Fight Goes On

Martin Luther King holds up photographs of the three missing campaigners at a meeting in Mississippi in 1964.

In the state of Mississippi, three civil rights workers went missing after being arrested in June 1964. King went to Mississippi to support a campaign for blacks to be awarded the voting rights that were theirs by law. The missing men's bodies were found two weeks after he arrived.

King knew that his own life was also in danger, but he refused to cancel his trip.

'**The battle was far from won. It had only begun.**'
King, writing about the problems that still faced blacks after the 1964 Civil Rights Act had been passed.

While King campaigned in Mississippi, President Lyndon Johnson, who had taken over when President Kennedy was assassinated, campaigned in the 1964 presidential elections. Johnson, a Democrat, supported civil rights. His Republican opponent, Barry Goldwater, was less keen on the changes that had taken place in the United States.

King could not resist adding his powerful voice to the debate. He spoke out against Goldwater, urging blacks and whites to vote for Johnson so that the march towards equality could continue.

Johnson won the election. But King's high-profile role in politics was making him more enemies than ever.

Thousands of blacks and whites joined King on another huge march, the March against Fear, in Mississippi in 1966.

The Nobel Prize

After years of struggles, successes and setbacks, King had worn himself out. In October 1964, he checked into hospital suffering from exhaustion.

The next morning he received a phone call from Coretta. He had been announced as the winner of the 1964 Nobel Peace Prize. This prize, one of the most prestigious in the world, is awarded every year to the person who has done the most for peace and friendship anywhere in the world. King was honoured and greatly moved. At last the whole world was listening to his dream.

'I fought hard to hold back the tears ... Whatever I was, I owed to my family and to all those who struggled with me. But the biggest debt I owed to my wife.'
King remembering his feelings of pride and gratitude when he accepted the 1964 Nobel Peace Prize.

King and his wife Coretta hug each other at a press conference held to announce that he had won the Nobel Peace Prize.

King proudly holds the Nobel Peace Prize Gold Medal, awarded to him in 1964.

In December, King went to Oslo in Norway for the award ceremony. In his acceptance speech, he said that he was accepting the prize on behalf of the 'unknown ground crew' — the millions of ordinary people who had taken part in peaceful protests. He also called for an end to racial injustice, poverty and war around the world.

The Last Years

King never wavered from his belief in non-violence. But some blacks were growing tired of enduring violent racist attacks without retaliating.

One of these was a black Muslim leader named Malcolm X. In the early 1960s, he encouraged black people to fight violence with violence. Unlike King, Malcolm X thought blacks should demand their own political power and run their lives separately from whites. Malcolm X was assassinated in 1965, but a new movement, with the slogan 'Black Power', picked up on his ideas.

'I have often wished that he would talk less of violence, because violence is not going to solve our problem.' King on his fellow black leader Malcolm X.

King met with Malcolm X, but did not agree with all his ideas.

Violence erupted in Watts, a suburb of Los Angeles, when crowds of angry blacks rioted and set fire to buildings.

This made King very unhappy. He wanted people of all races to come together in love and friendship, not take sides. He was afraid the Black Power movement would frighten white people and reinforce racist hatred.

So, as the Black Power movement grew, King carried on his peaceful work. He campaigned for civil rights in Selma, Alabama, and against poverty in Chicago. He also spoke out against the US involvement in the Vietnam War, believing as always that peaceful negotiations would work better than bombs.

King arriving in his old home town of Montgomery after a march in 1965.

Death at the Motel Lorraine

King's last campaign was called the Poor People's Campaign. It was organized in 1967 by the Southern Christian Leadership Conference to help poor people of all races demand jobs and fair pay. King and the SCLC's other leaders planned to hold more massive, non-violent protests like the March on Washington, which had been a huge success in 1963.

Right up until his death, King was taking part in the huge civil rights marches which were now common across the South.

Martin Luther King and two friends Jesse Jackson (left) and Ralph Abernathy (right) stand on the balcony at the Motel Lorraine in Memphis, where he was assassinated just a day after this photo was taken. The bullet seemed to come from the guest house opposite the motel.

'Like anybody, I would like to live a long life – longevity has its place. But I'm not concerned about that now. I just want to do God's will. And He's allowed me to go up to the mountain. And I've looked over, and I've seen the Promised Land. I may not get there with you. But I want you to know tonight, that we, as a people, will get to the Promised Land. And so I'm happy tonight; I'm not worried about anything; I'm not fearing any man. Mine eyes have seen the glory of the coming of the Lord.'
King speaking to striking sanitation workers in Memphis, Tennessee, on 3 April 1968.

As part of the campaign, King went to Memphis, Tennessee to support the city's sanitation workers, who were on strike. On 3 April 1968, he made a strange speech to them in which he talked about his own life, saying it didn't matter to him how much longer he lived.

The following evening, as he stepped onto the balcony outside his room at the Motel Lorraine, King was knocked off his feet by a bullet fired from a guest house across the street. It had hit him in the chest, and he died almost immediately.

Who Did It?

James Earl Ray, shown in the inset photo, hiding his face as he is taken to prison in March 1969.

An escaped criminal named James Earl Ray was arrested and accused of King's murder. He confessed to the killing, pleaded guilty in court, and was sent to jail, where he stayed until his death in 1998.

An open and shut case? Some people think not. It turned out that Ray's lawyers had pressurized him to confess. Just a few days after pleading guilty, he withdrew his confession and said he had been framed.

Indeed, there are several clues that suggest Ray was not acting alone, and may not even have been the killer.

For example, witnesses claimed to have seen a gunman outside the guest house, even though the FBI (the Federal Bureau of Investigation, who investigated the murder) said Ray was inside it at the time of the shooting. The guest house owner said she did not recognize Ray as a customer. And Ray himself had been in the army, and was known to be a poor shot.

Members of Martin Luther King's family at his funeral in 1968.

So was there a conspiracy? It's still not clear. By the end of his life, King was a powerful leader, with many enemies. The Ku Klux Klan, the FBI or even someone in the government could have wanted to get rid of him. Nothing has ever been proved. But James Earl Ray protested his innocence until the end of his life.

> **Dexter Scott King: 'I just wanna ask you, for the record: erm, did you kill my father?'**
> **James Earl Ray: ' No, no I didn't, no.'**
> From a 1997 interview between Martin Luther King's son Dexter and James Earl Ray.

The Legacy

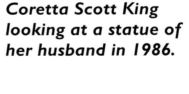

If you looked around a typical school, shopping mall, washroom (public toilets) or workplace in the USA today, you would see Americans of all races and backgrounds sharing the same space and the same facilities. Segregation is a thing of the past. Laws against racial prejudice have been passed, not just in the USA, but around the world.

So did Martin Luther King change the world? He claimed the civil rights movement would have happened anyway, whether he was there or not. But in him, the struggle had a unique leader — a man whose endless determination, passionate beliefs and astonishing speechmaking could move a whole nation to action.

Coretta Scott King looking at a statue of her husband in 1986.

MARTIN LUTHER KING, JR.

HUMANITARIAN

1929 - 1968

King died knowing that the battle was not over. Even today, prejudice still exists. There are still racist attacks, and there are still people who would rather judge others by the colour of their skin than by their character. But the world is gradually moving towards the ideal of complete equality, and the freedom that King firmly believed would one day come.

'I refuse to accept the view that mankind is so tragically bound to the starless midnight of racism and war that the bright daybreak of peace and brotherhood can never become a reality ...
I still believe that we shall overcome.'
King in his Nobel Prize acceptance speech, on 10 December 1964.

A boy holds a picture of Martin Luther King during a celebration held in Tennessee to mark the thirtieth anniversary of King's death.

Glossary

artery A large blood vessel.

assassin A killer who murders a famous person, usually on someone else's orders.

Baptist Church A branch of the Christian Church.

boycott To make a protest by refusing to buy a particular product or service.

caste system A traditional Indian system which divides society into many different levels.

conspiracy A secret plot or plan involving a number of people.

constitution A set of principles that define the way a country is run.

Democrat A member of the Democratic party, one of the USA's two main political parties.

desegregation The process of abolishing segregation.

federal To do with the government of the USA.

MIA (Montgomery Improvement Association) A society organized to run the bus boycott in Montgomery. Martin Luther King was its leader.

NAACP (National Association for the Advancement of Colored People) A national organization which campaigns against racism in the USA.

Republican A member of the Republican party, one of the USA's two main political parties.

SCLC (Southern Christian Leadership Conference) An organization led by Martin Luther King, which ran many civil rights campaigns.

segregation The system which forced blacks and whites to use separate facilities.

senator An elected member of the US Congress.

spiritual A religious song traditionally sung by black slaves.

Further Information

Books to read

Free at Last: The Story of Martin Luther King by Angela Bull (Dorling Kindersley Children's Books, 2000)

Lives and Times: Martin Luther King by Peter and Connie Roop (Heinemann, 2001)

Sources

The Autobiography of Martin Luther King, Jr. edited by Clayborne Carson (Abacus, 2000)

Martin Luther King Jr Papers Project Stanford University, USA Tel: 001 650 723 2092

Date Chart

1929, 15 January Michael (Martin) Luther King Jr born in Atlanta, Georgia, USA.

1944, 17 April Takes part in a public speaking contest in Dublin, Georgia.

1948, 14 September Goes to Crozer Seminary to train as a preacher.

1950, Spring Hears Mordecai Johnson give a lecture about Gandhi.

1951, 13 September Goes to Boston University to study theology.

1953, 8 June Marries Coretta Scott in Marion, Alabama.

1954, 31 October Takes up first job as a minister in Montgomery, Alabama.

1955, 17 November First child, Yolanda Denise, is born.

1955, 5 December Montgomery bus boycott begins.

1956, 13 November US Supreme Court rules that segregation is against the Constitution.

1957, 14 February Becomes leader of Southern Christian Leadership Conference (SCLC).

1957, March Travels to Ghana to witness independence celebrations.

1957, 23 October Second child, Martin Luther King III, is born.

1958, 20 September Is stabbed during a book signing in New York.

1959, February–March Travels around India and meets Prime Minister Nehru.

1960, 1 February Moves back to Atlanta, Georgia with family.

1961, 30 January Third child, Dexter Scott King, is born.

1963, 28 March Fourth child, Bernice Albertine, is born.

1963, April–May Leads civil rights campaign in Birmingham, Alabama.

1963, 28 August Gives 'I have a dream' speech in Washington DC.

1963, 15 September An explosion in a church in Birmingham kills four girls.

1963, 22 November President John F. Kennedy is assassinated in Dallas, Texas.

1964, 2 July Attends signing of the 1964 Civil Rights Act.

1964, 4 August Three civil rights workers are found murdered in Mississippi.

1964, November Democratic candidate Lyndon Johnson wins presidential election.

1964, 10 December King is awarded the Nobel Peace Prize in Oslo, Norway.

1965, 21 February Pro-violence black leader Malcolm X is assassinated in New York.

1965–1967 King repeatedly speaks out against American involvement in the Vietnam War.

1968, 4 April King is assassinated at the Motel Lorraine in Memphis, Tennessee.

Index

Page numbers in **bold** mean there is a picture on the page.